The Personification
of Change

The Personification of Change

of Change

Gary Nelson Wilkins

To order additional copies of this book, contact:
Xlibris Corporation
1-888-795-4274
www.Xlibris.com
Orders@Xlibris.com
43881

Contents

Preface...15

Chapter 1   President: Thomas Jefferson. But what is change? 19

Chapter 2   President: James Madison and how or what
            should we change?..35

Chapter 3   President: James Monroe But yet still,
            is there really change? 45

Summary...53

Presidents:

Jefferson, 1801-1809

Madison 1809-1817

And

Monroe 1817-1825

The third, fourth, and fifth presidents of the United States.

Acknowledgements

This manuscript is dedicated to the city of Richmond, Virginia, where I got to live for 2 (two) and a half years (Jan. 1991-april 1993).

My roommate was Greg Potter, a Vietnam veteran.

While in Richmond, Virginia I got to take the Mount Vernon tour for the fourth time and Montecello tour, Madison estate tour, and the Monroe estate tour one time.

You can not believe how nice of a time I had taking a tour of the presidents houses (estates)

The "the personification of change" or as the author might also have entitled this work the "the personification of man" is a work inclusive with—in the "the books (writings) of deism.

But as it is so the author has entitled the work the "the personification of change". For as it is for all seasons and for all times it is change.

It was also in Richmond, Virginia that I got to work at odd jobs and write my manuscript on Lewis and Clark.

Presidential Seal

1706-1790

BENJAMIN FRANKLIN

WRITES A LETTER IN HIS 84TH YEAR

TO HIS FRIEND

PRESIDENT GEORGE WASHINGTON

A Benjamin Franklin decision

Preface

The dawn breaks in the east. A new day begins, middles, and ends. A new baby boy or new baby girl is born day or night into this world. And an elderly man or woman pass away day or night in this world. This is as is added too or as is subtracted from in the United States.

But what is change?

And how or what should we change?

But yet still is there really change?

For true self-government means change.

Change for everyone.

Self-government should be your first and or your second wind. A testament of courage to all. Like a lighthouse in the fog at sea. Self-government is the responsibility of each and every person in the nation.

The citizen state and now since 1959.

There are some 50 states in the union. (United States)

You are a resident of the state you live in. And you are a citizen of the country you live in. *One citizen/one state

For: for the author in our fast paced society and world (of nuclear holocaust) its "what you stand for" when you die and "who you die with" when you die that's important.

*note: "The Eternal Ones": there is "one" eternal one for each universe. "one" eternal one for "one" universe. This numbers out into infinity.

President:
1801-1809

President
Thomas Jefferson
Third president of the United States

Chapter 1

President: Thomas Jefferson.
But what is change?

Therefore we begin, middle, and end our dissertation with the hypothetical math equation or formula:

$$\frac{C = RG \cdot rp}{S} \quad RP$$

Where as:

C: is change
=:   equals
RG: real growth
RP: relative to proximity
S: in seconds
RP: with real power

But again what is change?

For a man, woman, or child can change spiritually, mentally and/or physically over-night at their own speed. (Pace)

Furthermore:

Is the "The Self" (oxygen and lungs) and the "the little self" (food, drink and stomach) the only tools by which men and women can fight to change their lives?

Change the way in which they live? Or is a man or woman tied to their heredity or their environment without mercy?

Physically speaking:

Proper food and drink makes for the strong growth of bones and a healthy body.

But change is the reorganizations of the metabolism of man and woman.

And with huge amounts of oxygen and proper food is a catalyst for the proper cell division in the body of man and woman attainable.

Again this is accomplished by breathing the largest amount of oxygen you can breath into your lungs and the correct diet of food in the stomach.

(The Self/the little self)

A fight to change your life. Therefore the correct equation is:

$$O = F \,\&\, D$$

O:	is oxygen
=:	equals
F & d:	is food and drink

- Is change: therefore;
- A correct, pleasant, or normal-behavior, personality, or attitude.
- The improvement of man or woman(s) character?
- Being a better person, better man or woman, or better nation of people.
- A more capable man or woman.
- Self-reliant & proud.
- Or a mind, body or spirit full of sunlight? (darkness at death)
- Or simply a different person? (change of countenance)
- And or up on the scale of evolution.

Spiritually speaking:
(For the author change is).

- [ ] Consistent and constructive.
- [ ] Change is a man or woman's birth—right!
- [ ] Change is always done by a leader chosen by the people. (vote)
- [ ] And change is always done by a man or woman who lives in the future.

In addition:

Physically, mentally, and spiritually the "The Self" (oxygen & lungs) harbors every diversion or distraction in man or woman(s) heart.

(Men and women)

When breathing through the mouth

Meditation for the brain and mind

But then what is change?

Change is also expansion!

For the correct path to enlightenment will always be to meditate on the "The Self" (oxygen) as it enters, fills, and expands the lungs. Oxygen is then added to the blood stream. The heart pumps the oxygen in the blood straight up the main artery(s) that leads to the brain. The oxygen in the blood is then combined with the neurons in the brain. The brain then distributes the oxygen in the blood stream to all parts of the body. Like its supposed to be done. And the gray and white matter in the brain goes up and down the spinal column.

Sunlight: activity

Darkness: sleep (dreams)

Air, oxygen, & wind, (The Self)

Food and drink (the little self)

Occasional sexual intercourse (with heterosexuals) (wife)

And what ever else is desired (talking with other people) should be at the forefront of the brain. Consciousness. Fresh air is the God head at the forefront of the brain. *(mind)

*in the summer months:

A family, friends, or relatives who spread a blanket on the grass in a public park with a picnic basket full of food and drink and have a picnic sitting on the grass is an excellent idea on how to understand what the "The Self" (oxygen) and the "the little self" (food and drink) does in the metabolism of man, woman or child (or on a picnic table, camping, or at the ocean beach or a river bank.)

When breathing through the nostrils only you can imagine the oxygen going straight up through the sinus(es) to the forefront of the brain. (mind)

The endocrine glands also play an important part in maintaining the health of the body. (hormones are based on food & drink)

When the universe is gone so is the "The Eternal One" is gone with it also. (non-being)

Macrocosm and microcosm.
So it is written:

God breathes in and out as the (this) universe expands.

Thus a man or woman can see their I.Q. Expand in school or at college.

Man and woman can see their bodies grow and expand in life.
(animals, plants, and minerals also expand.)

Man and woman(s) digestive system (tract) stomach expands.

Man and woman's genitals expand.

And a woman(s) belly expands when she is pregnant.

Cell division is also expansion.

The universes don't move or travel through outer space. The universes just expand*.

In the opinion of the author the "one male cell" came into being in the form or image of oxygen.

And (two) the "one female cell" came into being in the form or image of food and drink.

But I guess man and woman came into being in the form or image of God and Goddess and the "The Eternal One(s)".

*according to modern science the "universe(s)" would expand with an infinite amount of matter

In this temporal

Existence the universes number out into infinity. There is one God and Goddess for each universe and one eternal one for each universe.

However:

The "The Eternal One(s)" are one. The universes are separate. But the "The Eternal One" is one. The "The Eternal One" is one for all the separate universes!

The proper cell division of man and woman:

The proper amount of oxygen, food, and drink consumed by the cell(s) makes cell division possible. If organisms or creatures lived forever there wouldn't be enough oxygen or food & drink to go around.

The "The Eternal Ones" are "one"!

"one" eternal "one" for each universe.

In life:

Life begins as a one cell organism or one cell creature.

Then life is one (one male cell) and two (one female cell) at the same time.
(cell division)
(male and female cell division)

What has evolved is "two" entirely different or separate (male & female) celled organisms or creatures.

Then life's population: (male & female)

Then cells divide into one (cell) and many (cells) at the same time. This is in the body of the organisms or creatures (male & female) and as organisms and creatures multiply in sexual reproduction.

(One and many)

Organisms and creatures

In the universe(s) there is one God as a being for each universe. Then there are God and Goddess one and two at the same time. And then Gods and Goddesses one and many at the same time for each of the universes. (Matter and space)

That exists!

There is one God/one Goddess matter and space for each separate universe. There is "one eternal one" for all the separate universes.

And the universes number out into infinity!

According to the "The Eternal One" in order of existence God is a being, God is a vehicle. God commutes or travels thru the universe (outer space) like a bird soars in flight.

(This is from star to star; galaxy to galaxy; solar system to solar system; and planets to planets.)

The universe(s) expand(s)

The universe(s) do not move or travel. The "The Eternal Ones" have put forth beings throughout outer space that with the proper skill and or know how move or travel thru outer space and reality changes hands. Sometimes Gods in the universes gang up on the "The Eternal One" the Gods trying to defeat the "The Eternal Ones."

However the Gods come into being and are a vehicle. (one and many) this from the "The Eternal Ones" and the Gods return to the "The Eternal One" when their time is up at death. (non-being)

("The Eternal One" walks through the intellect.)

The intellects walk together.

God goes back to a collection of Gods.

All the "The Eternal One(s) do is spend all their time bringing Gods thru to a temporal existence and all they get for it is being ganged up on. But God does run the universe(s) and knows how its supposed to be run.

(not the intellect)

The universe(s) is not a bad account.

However the senses the "The Eternal One" sees thru each living creature. Not the rest of the "The Eternal One" does that all by themselves alone.

(Intellect, senses, word(s), and reality.)

The "eternal" is the long way to go.

For it is written: the "eternal" sees through all creatures and partakes of a meal that way. (living matter) and God teaches or shows man how to find or get a meal for himself. This is living matter. A vehicle for all. Or how to take a breath of fresh air for himself.

The "eternal" said: I am the life in every living creature that exists. And God is their vehicle. God is a vehicle. God is a being. God is the first being in the order of existence as far back as you can go in creation before you reach the "eternal".

But for the author it is not clear what food God eats or consumes.

And the "eternal" said that all living creatures are junk unless God functions as a vehicle.

And God said: that when you get a meal for yourself you don't ask questions!

Finally:

A God, the "The Eternal One" and the monolithic maximum of change.

But what is change?

The "The Eternal One" comes down out of the sky into being and returns up into the sky after being.

The "eternal" is being.

The "eternal" is one.

And then one and two at the same time.

And then again

One and many at the same time.

This is for each universe.

"The Eternal One"

There are different stars; solar systems with planets; and different universes with similar male and female life forms that live on those planets.

The "eternal" comes into being (life) and comes out of being (death) all the time.

The "The Eternal Ones" also like God enjoy traveling thru outer space like a bird soars in flight. (soars in the air!)

God and the "The Eternal Ones" get a meal for themselves like all other creatures do. But the author is not sure what is eaten. Probably pure matter is consumed. The "The Eternal One" was created by its own vehicle.

"I am solid vehicle!"

The sun

Our star: to hot and to bright a light to handle.

186,282 miles per second (medium traveling speed)

The speed of light. There are different speeds at which to travel at through the galaxy(s) universe and universes.

The "The Eternal Ones" (I) travel faster then the speed of light.

The "The Eternal Ones" (I) was created (their vehicles) to travel faster then the speed of light that way. The "eternal" was created or come into being that way.

First ladies 1801-1809

Thomas Jefferson's daughters and
Dolly Madison acted as first ladies. (Hostess)

1748-1782

Mrs. Jefferson
(No portrait in existence)

President: 1809-1817

President
James Madison
Fourth president of the United States

Chapter 2

President: James Madison and how or what should we change?

Man, woman, and child were meant to put forth effort and to make strides in the following fields of endeavor: (only unto what is real change and years of truth for oneself.)

Category(s):	ages:
1. Religion	(1-65 to death)
2. Infants:	(children 1-12)
* 3. Puberty:	(13-18)
4. Adults/marriage:	(18-65)
5. Parents/parenting:	(18-65) (18-30)
6. Politics:	(18-20-25-35-65)
7. Old age:	(65-death)

(retirement)

* (primary-secondary sexual characteristics)

1. Religion

The soul:

For the author religion is the personification of change in the awareness of the spirit in a man, woman, or child's body. This is change spiritually, mentally, and or physically.

This is the degree of which awareness of the "The Eternal Ones" and of God is as the spirit involves all things that pertains to the spiritual world. (everything)

This is accomplished by (one) breathing "The Self" (the most oxygen large or largest lung capacity) that you can breathe. And the "the little self" proper food and drink. (this is your fare share of proper food and drink.) This is also the degree of spiritual awareness that exists covered over by bad living habits and or a bad life style, as God and the "eternal" is not.

2. Infants/children

Orientation/disorientation

Ages 1-12 years

The author does not profess to be a child psychologist, however what determines a normal functioning child's brain is usually whether he or she is oriented or disoriented.

This later in life determines whether the child is centered or not as an adult.

3. Puberty

Sex education

Ages 13-18 years

The author considers the key or main words in puberty to be that of *sex education*.

This involves some anatomy terminology mixed in with some street language and the young man or young woman seeing the changes for themselves that take place in their own bodies.

How to use (common sense)

4. Adults/marriage

Ages: (18-65)

Marriage for the author is a union between a man and a woman in holy matrimony.

A man and woman each day begin, middle, and end with each other in all matters that start with their wedding and carry on till their deaths. It's a bond that exists everyday of their lives between each other throughout all of their lives as married couples.

A married man and woman also bring children into this world. (responsibly)

5. Parents/parenting

Ages: (18-65 males)
Ages: (18-30 females)

Parents to the author are a man and woman who sexually bring a boy or girl child into this world through birth and raise them to be adults.

This is done by giving them room and space to breathe and to grow and providing them with a system of meals, plus education, and spiritual teachings. (Religion)

6. Politics

Ages: (18-20-25-35-65)

A political philosophy the citizen state:

The author believes that nobody owns the "the state" a persons finances are done by a privately owned bank or banker usually run by the state veterans.

(this is as the "the state" exists)

To the author the ideal basic governmental political philosophy would be as follows *

Caution: in the United States it is simply based on the democratic party and the republican party. Different political or non-political party affiliation.
*6. Politics

(a.)   The
       National
       Democratic
       Capitalists
       Party
       Of America

A multiple or multi-affiliation political party

   (A)   One political party caucus members.
   (B)   The conservative party
   (C)   The liberal party
   (D)   Numerous or non-political party affiliation

(18 years old until retirement)

7. Old age

Retirement

Ages: 65 to death

The author considers old age and retirement to be society's way of treating an elderly man or woman after they have worked all of their life.

The children of the elderly people taking care of them or being sent to a rest home when they can't take care of themselves anymore.

An elderly man or woman might also be treated with a lot of respect.

And how or what should we change? Again.

Change is existence:

Two come thru the universes such a long or far distance that you can not even imagine it.

Two come thru the universes to do work. This work is to base everything on one.

But a third party said that everything is based on two.

Is everything based on one? Or is everything based on two?

Everyone has decided that it's a combination of the two. (two and one!)

There is one "eternal one" for each universe.

According to the "eternal one(s)" its possible for man (human beings) technologically to travel thru space faster then the speed of light. The "The Eternal One" (I) was sitting there and then (I) figured out that I was just there.

And then (I) "The Eternal One" found out who I am. And then I just traveled thru the universes that way.

I "The Eternal One" do a lot of things in this universe besides partake of a meal. (I) am a very proud bird! ("The Eternal One")

(I) "The Eternal Ones" comes into being that way.

(It's difficult to explain)

There was a flash of light and then "The Eternal Ones" were traveling faster then the speed of light thru the universes.

They "The Eternal Ones" come into being that way.

There is one "eternal one" for each universe.

(As stated before)

The "eternal one" travels at its own speed and this is at its own leisure. The scheme of things for this universe came into being with in seconds at (in) Gods time frame.

First lady 1809-1817

**First lady
Mrs. Madison**

President: 1817-1825

President
James Monroe
Fifth President of the United States

Chapter 3

President: James Monroe But yet still, is there really change?

The correct frame or state of mind in which to change is that of a clean and or a clear mind.

(with little or no fantasies.)

A dream that turns into goals in life and then reality for oneself and a restful sleep at night. The important attitude in the mind to have when it is to change is resolve and with other people or by oneself do we change.

Well, of course there is real change in a democracy with a capitalistic economic system of private property ownership for all.

This is truly what the millennium holds for everybody man, woman, and child.

It's like listening and playing classical music for the millennium.

(I) "The Eternal One" put the universe here thru man! Is the "The Eternal One(s)" are they male or female? "The Eternal One(s)" are neither male nor female

I am pure light! (No temperature)

A cell (body) is based on one! All celestial or heavenly bodies—stars, (suns), planets, comets, moons, asteroids, and black holes are based on one. A star is based on one. A universe is based on one, meteorites too. This is in outer space. (One and many).

The "eternal one" knows exactly the number and what universe(s) were here before this (our) universe was here.

And the "eternal one" has already planned out what and the number of universe(s) that are here in our space after (our) this universe is gone. (out of existence)

A yellow color:

A collection of different items in this universe (old) are refurbished or (recycled if you will) take in for the new universe(s).

(I) the "eternal one" are refurbishing a collection of different items while at the same time (I) am maintaining (the) this universe(s).

In the brain (mind) a reticular formation

India-China (the Far East) and Greece.

The lungs and stomach exercise, meditation, and work out.

Consciousness is handed down from generation to generation along with the subconscious mind.

Therefore unless you study with a real legitimate swami a guru, a oriental master at martial arts, or an amateur or professional athlete.

These are merely yoga breathing and posture disciplines, self defense techniques, and calisthenics exercises that don't really leave or make a lasting impression on the individual. You have to stick with it until graduation. For most of us a (the) novice (by the book) respiratory meditation.

"The Self" (lungs)

It takes huge amounts of oxygen to maintain life, movement, and thought. The lungs receive a full and thorough work out and exercise when the following occurs.

This is considered deep breathing:

1. What (I'm) going to do!
2. "What (I) should have done"
3. "And what (I) will do!"

Digestive meditation

"the little self" (stomach)

When you eat an entire meal for yourself your stomach, large intestines, and small intestines receive a full and complete work out and exercise for themselves.

(no additional work is really necessary. It must be proper food and drink.)

However eating a meal and being active for the day is important.
The lungs and stomach should receive a rest during sleep at night.

Neurons
Respiratory muscles
Digestive muscles

The forefront

(Memory and association)

Just about anything comes to the forefront of the brain or mind.

1. The Eternal One
2. God
3. Goddess
4. A beginning, middle, and end.
5. Air, oxygen, and wind
6. Food and drink
7. Pain
8. Pleasure
9. The opposite sex
10. Sexual intercourse
11. Work
12. Occupation
13. Profession
14. Dreams
15. Sleep
16. Marriage
17. Rest
18. Etc., etc., etc.,

First lady 1817-1825

**First lady
Mrs. Monroe**

Summary

Poetry in motion:

To live in the hills, to not be ill, the knowledge of the wise, but still yet compromised, the founding fathers that founded the government healed the people from repugnance, a beginning, middle, and an end on their own, these people in the United States finally call their country: home, to be called a warrior or a diplomat spread the government strong but fast heaven or hell will it last, the people the change is near, the millenniums gone by an honest past, a brain with arms and legs of an army, stick together like that in harmony, go forth by yourself then an adult man or woman, save yourself from a peril or a burden, the millenniums seem as though they are nothing, quiet and still like that of an army.

Don't forget the (3) three primordial body positions (postures) as first mentioned in the bible:

Standing up (walking)

Sitting down (chair)

Lying down (bed)

All movement originates from these (3) three body positions. (postures)

You begin, middle, and end all movement from these (3) three body positions.

*meals: a picnic is for both sexes.

Your family, friends, and relatives always eat a meal on a wooden dinner table with wooden chairs and the appropriate utensils: fork, knife, spoon, plate, dish, bowls, cups, and glasses.

The personification of change was finished in the 48th year of my life.

2/16/2007

Author:

Gary Nelson Wilkins

*federal: (fed-all the people a meal) government.

As the author brings this work to an end. I suppose a husband might change for his wife and or a wife might change for her husband in a relationship or marriage. This is as is the personification of change.

Cattle: bulls and cows, hogs and pigs, horses, roosters, chickens, and dogs, turkeys, goats, sheep, cats, deers and moose's (elk), bears and wolves, birds, buffalo.

Deism (customs and culture)

A ranch: according to the religion of deism, and it's folklore, and followers: all domestic farm animals and all wildlife animals should be allowed to die of natural causes and then be taken to a slaughterhouse to be made into food and trophies.

Unless they are a danger to the public.

The public should always remember to eat a lot of whole wheat bread, vegetables, fruit, and a variety of foods and drinks with their meat (meals).

Some high-lights in the life of Thomas Jefferson.

- Thomas Jefferson 1743-1826
- Graduated: William and Mary College. Lawyer
- Author: the declaration of independence
- Governor of Virginia
- Congressman
- Minister to France
- Secretary of state (Washington)
- Vice President (Adams)
- President: 1801-1809

As president

- Tripoli declared war on America
- West point opened
- The Louisiana purchase
- The Lewis and Clark expedition
- The Jefferson bible
- Founded university of Virginia

Monticello
Home of
Thomas Jefferson

Montecello

Some high-lights in the life of James Madison.

- James Madison 1751-1836
- Graduated: Princeton university
- Interested in politics
- Father of the constitution
- Virginia assemblyman
- Constitutional convention
- Congressman
- Secretary of state (Jefferson)
- President: 1809-1817

As president:

- War of 1812

The Madison estate

Some high-lights in the life of James Monroe.

- James Monroe 1758-1831
- Attended William and Mary college
- Joined the army
- A lieutenant
- Virginia assembly
- State politics
- U.S. Senator
- Governor of Virginia
- Secretary of state
- President: 1817-1825

As president

- The Monroe Doctrine

The Permanence of Oak Hill

Former Estate of President James Monroe

The Monroe Estate